WOLVES

WOLVES

MICHAEL GEORGE

THE CHILD'S WORLD

DESIGN
Bill Foster of Albarella & Associates, Inc.

PHOTO CREDITS
Jim Brandenburg: back cover, 11, 16, 19, 20, 23, 24, 26, 29, 30
Tom and Pat Leeson: front cover, 2, 9, 13
W. Perry Conway: 6
Joe McDonald: 15

Distributed to schools and libraries
in Canada by
SAUNDERS BOOK CO.
Collingwood, Ontario, Canada L9Y 3Z7
(800) 461-9120

Library of Congress Cataloging-in-Publication Data
George, Michael, 1964-
Wolves/Michael George.
p. cm. — (Child's World Wildlife Library)
Summary: Discusses the characteristics and behavior of
the wolf, one of the most endangered animals in the world.
ISBN 0-89565-711-2
1. Wolves — Juvenile literature.   [1. Wolves.]   I. Title.
II. Series.   91-12507
QL737.C22G47 1991   CIP
599.74'442—dc20   AC

Dedicated to the return of wolves to Yellowstone National Park

A re you afraid of the big, bad wolf? If so, you are not alone. Many people think that wolves are mean, evil creatures. Some people think wolves like to eat humans, just like in the story "Little Red Riding Hood." In real life, however, wolves are very different from the animals in the stories we've heard.

Wolves look like big dogs. A large male wolf can be three feet tall and over six feet long. He can weigh more than 100 pounds. Although wolves look like dogs, they cannot be kept as pets. Wolves are wild animals. They do not like to be cooped up and fed. They prefer to roam free and hunt for food.

Throughout history, people have always misunderstood wolves. People heard wolves howl at night. They saw wolf tracks near the remains of large animals. People thought that wolves were vicious animals. They believed that wolves would kill anything, even people.

Horror stories made people afraid of wolves. Many people wanted all the wolves in the world to be killed. We became the wolf's worst enemy. We trapped, shot, and poisoned millions of wolves.

Two hundred years ago, there were at least 2 million wolves in North America alone. Today only about 30,000 wolves remain. One type of wolf that lives in North America is the red wolf. Unfortunately, only about 50 red wolves still live in the wild. They are one of the most endangered animals in the world.

The only other type of wolf that lives in North America is the gray wolf. Gray wolves can live anyplace where they can find enough food. They live in mountainous areas, marshlands, forests, and open plains.

Despite their name, gray wolves can be almost any color. Most often they are shades of black, gray, or brown. Some gray wolves that live in the Far North are pure white. The color of a wolf's fur blends in with its surroundings. People and other animals have to look carefully to see a wolf.

Gray wolves have warm, woolly fur. Their fur can be three inches thick during the winter. A wolf's thick fur works like a raincoat. Rain and snow easily run off the wolf's body so its skin stays dry. The only part of a wolf not covered with fur is its nose. To keep their noses warm, wolves curl up into little balls. They tuck their noses under their furry tails.

Most wolves live in groups called *packs*. Wolf packs vary in size. Some packs have only one male and one female. Large packs may have as many as 25 wolves.

Each wolf pack has one leader. The leader is usually the oldest male. He may be the biggest wolf in the pack. However, even a small wolf can be the leader 's smart.

A wolf pack is really just a family of wolves. The leader and his mate are the father and mother. Their babies are the youngest members of the pack. The other wolves are brothers, sisters, or other close relatives.

The members of a wolf family are very close friends. They play together and nuzzle each other. The older wolves help to raise the young. They act as babysitters, teachers, and playmates.

Although wolves cannot talk like people, they do communicate. The pack leader howls when he wants the family to come together. Wolves whimper to greet each other. They also whimper when they are sad. A growl means "stay away" or "behave!" A bark tells the other wolves that something is wrong. Sometimes a family of wolves howls together just for the fun of it!

A wolf pack does not always just sit around and have fun. The members also work together to capture food. One wolf is strong, but a pack of wolves is much stronger. They can catch animals that are much bigger than they are.

When wolves are searching for food they trot at about five miles per hour. They can trot over 50 miles without resting. When they spot a meal, however, wolves put on the speed. They can run up to 40 miles per hour. That's twice as fast as you can ride a bicycle!

Wolves are not picky eaters. They like many different kinds of food. They prefer to eat large, plant-eating animals such as deer, mountain sheep, and caribou. They also like moose, elk, and buffalo. If food is hard to find, they will eat rabbits, birds, and even mice.

People used to think that wolves killed animals just for fun. However, wolves kill only the animals that they need to eat. In addition, they prefer to hunt weak, old, or sick animals. In this way, wolves actually help animal populations. Only the strongest animals survive and produce healthy offspring.

There are some things that wolves don't eat. They do not normally eat horses, cattle, or sheep. Wolves usually stay away from farms and ranches. They fear people and sneak away before we can see them. Wolves also do not eat humans. Each year, more people are struck by lightning than have ever been attacked by wolves!

Wolves are not the creatures that are described in fairy tales. They are not mean, bloodthirsty killers and they do not eat people. Instead, wolves are intelligent and gentle animals. They are important and valuable members of the wilderness.